THE ULTIMATE GUIDE TO MARKETING YOUR GYM

Vince Gabriele, MS

THE ULTIMATE GUIDE TO MARKETING YOUR GYM
by VINCENT GABRIELE

© 2018 by Vincent Gabriele.
All international and U.S. rights reserved.

This book may not be copied, or stored in any information retrieval system, in whole or in part, without permission in writing from the author.

For information write to: 63 Industrial Road
Berkeley Heights, New Jersey 07922
908-464-4441
WWW.GABRIELEFITNESS.COM

Printed in the United States of America
by BISTIPRESS
Union, New Jersey

For Marlene Gabriele, an incredible person

Praise for Vince Gabriele and The Ultimate Guide to Marketing Your Gym

"If you take Vince's approaches to work, your newly honed marketing muscles will get oohs and aaahs from colleagues and competitors alike! If you're looking to increase your sales and operate at ever higher levels of effectiveness, buy, read and use this book asap!"

— **Ari Weinzweig, Founder Zingerman's Deli**

"Anything you can learn from Vince, in my eyes, is gold."

— **Eric Cressey**

"I've watched Vince develop first an amazing business and then second, a niche as a mentor and business coach. Vince is rapidly becoming a go-to guy for fitness business info"

— **Michael Boyle**

"Vince is one of the best young fitness business consultants to come about in the last 20 years and has created one of the best training gyms in the country"

— **Thomas Plummer Founder of The National Fitness Business Alliance**

"Vince has given you a blueprint to build your own marketing machine in the following pages. Read and learn. More importantly, apply"

— **Pat Rigsby**

"Being in the industry a long time, it's refreshing to hear clear, practical, and authentic information on how to grow your fitness business. Vince boils down years of experience into simple steps fitness business owners can take to grow their business and impact more people."
— **Brett Klika**
IDEA Personal Trainer of the Year and Founder of SPIDERfit

"Take it from a guy who has been there, grown that. Vince isn't just a guy who has read a bunch of books about how to grow a business, he has actually DONE it."
— **Brian Sipotz**

"I had the good fortune to meet Vince in late 2012. It is no coincidence that it was also at that point where my business started to become robust and turn into what I had always wanted it to be. There aren't many people out there that understand the complexities of both the numbers and the emotions of owning a fitness business; however, Vince is one of those rare gems. I owe a great deal of my own personal success and the success of Newell Strength to Vince! I recommend that you shut up and listen anytime you have a chance to learn from him!"
— **Kyle Newell**
6-year client of Vince's

"Vince's Mentoring Program is an absolute success. In a world where seemingly every piece of business information can be Googled, there is still great knowledge that can only be gained through personal experience. Vince's Mentorship program is the best example of that. I went from a passionate yet exhausted coach, to a confident leader, strategically planning and influencing a dynamic team with a 35% ROI."

— **Brandon Kelly**
4-year client of Vince's

"As a financial consultant in the fitness industry, I have seen first-hand, Vince grow into one of the most profitable and successful gyms in the country! He has gone through it all and always delivers an insightful and honest opinion that will help you build a better business and a better life. This is a great resource and a must for all fitness professionals."

— **Michael Waldron**
CFO to many of the top gyms in America

"What the industry needs more of is straight talkers like Vince Gabriele. He's a no-nonsense business coach for gym owners that want what's working now, what's going to always work, and what's going to make them profitable this year."

— **Vito La Fata,**
founder of Fitness Profit Systems

"It is also very exciting that his messages and energy are going to reach far more people in and out of the fitness profession. When anyone's reach can extend to names and faces we will never know or see, it is a very special endeavor and from one that so many will benefit. Enjoy the Gabriele Energy!"

— **Charlie Weingroff**

CONTENTS

Foreword — ix
Introduction — 1

PART 1: THE BIG PICTURE STRATEGY

Chapter 1: Your Member Avatar — 7
Chapter 2: Using the Right Bait — 13
Chapter 3: The Execution Plan — 22
Chapter 4: Your Marketing Scoreboard — 27

PART 2: THE TACTICS

Chapter 5: The Referral Engine — 35
Chapter 6: Grassroots Marketing: A Forgotten Art That's Timeless — 42
Chapter 7: Core Events — 66
Chapter 8: Email Marketing Machine — 89
Chapter 9: Social Media Content — 94
Chapter 10: Paid Advertising — 99
Conclusion — 115

FOREWORD

Fitness business owners are an interesting group. We're not like most other entrepreneurs. We build our businesses based on what we know and enjoy. While this may seem normal in a landscape where phrases like 'follow your passion' get tossed around, but in reality, it's not.

You don't see guys who are grilling burgers on their back deck decide that they're just going to up and open a McDonalds and the entrepreneur who owns a half-dozen Sport Clips locations didn't get into it because he was excited about cutting hair.

No, for small business owners, we're different. And while being different has its share of advantage, it also often means that those who choose to open and operate a fitness business don't have an extensive background in business or marketing.

Gym owners may be great at getting results for their clients…but all too often they're not great at getting those clients in the first place. That's where this book and Vince Gabriele come in.

Vince entered this professional like many of us. An athlete whose college career had come to an end, but who wasn't ready to move away from fitness and performance being a big part of his life, Vince started as an employee and then transitioned to business owner after learning the profession.

That's about the time I got to know Vince and it was quickly apparent that he was different than most fitness business owners. Rather than taking the route most take when they open a gym and basically become a self-employed service provider, Vince built a truly out standing business.

He built a team, implemented effective processes and created a culture that his clients raved about. But perhaps the most impressive system he developed was centered around marketing.

In an industry where most business owners either rely on a single 'flavor of the week' marketing channel or just pass on doing much marketing at all, Vince has developed a multi-faceted approach to consistently bring in quality prospects month after month, using both effective online tactics and proven offline approaches.

This approach has allowed him to consistently grow year after year, regardless of changes to Facebook, economic downturns or unexpected life circumstances that took his attention elsewhere.

Imagine having a marketing machine that produced a steady flow of qualified leads like the one Vince has developed. How much easier would running your business become? How much less stress would you have? How much more income would you personally earn? Well, you don't have to imagine it because it's all right here. Vince has given you a blueprint to build your own marketing machine in the following pages. Read and learn. More importantly, apply.

Effective marketing may be the biggest obstacle stand-

Foreword

ing in the way of success for most businesses in our industry, but if you take action on what you learn in this book it won't be an obstacle for you any longer.

Pat Rigsby
Founder of over 25 different fitness
businesses PatRigsby.com

INTRODUCTION

It was 4:30 PM, I was on the turf running a consultation for a middle school athlete and his father was there with me. I was watching the kid run up and down the turf, having a conversation with the dad about his son. I knew I was going to close both of them that day. The son to our Sports Performance Program, the dad to our Adult Fitness.

About ½ way into the consultation, I saw the look on our office manager, Karen's, face, one I had never seen before. She said, "Vince come to the phone." I shrugged it off, told her to take a message and I would call back when I was done closing. She insisted I come to the phone. One of our coaches took over the consult and I took the call. It was my wife.

She had a panicked tone in her voice and told me to get in my car, pick her up and head to NYU hospital. Something was wrong with my dad. My father had a very bad stroke and was in brain surgery for close to 6 hours, the doctors working hard to remove a clot from his brain. He survived, but barely. He then had to get emergency heart surgery only a few days later. Things were not looking good.

This was the most challenging time of my life. In an instant, the entire dynamic of my family completely changed. I was broken. I was not able to focus on anything other than taking care of my mom, being there for my sisters and helping my family make life and death decisions.

I did not go to my gym for an entire month and was mentally gone for several more. But, something happened with my gym, something great. We continued to grow. The month this happened was a record month, the following months after we continued to hit our growth goal. All of this happened with the leader of the business essentially gone. I realized that my business finally gave me the ability to live the life I wanted. To spend more time with my family, to be able to be there when they truly needed me, to have freedom of time and money, to be able to focus on what I truly wanted.

Despite the awful situation that my family was in, I was never more proud of the gym I had built than I was then. My gym gave me this moment. My gym gave me the ability to step up and be with my family when they truly needed me. My mission is to give this opportunity to you, to build a gym that gives you the freedom you want.

I hope and pray that instead of driving into NYU hospital everyday … you realize this freedom on the beach with your family. The chapters that follow are the starting point to this life. It's hard to create a business that truly gives you freedom without a consistent reliable method to bring in new members. Nothing is truly necessary in a business if you don't have people paying you money. This is the foundation. This is marketing.

An education in marketing is the most important knowledge you need to give to attain the freedom that most gym owners truly want. I'm honored you're reading this book and hope you will join my mission of helping you create the life you desire from the fruits of your fitness business. I'm a personal trainer turned gym owner, just like you.

I do not have a huge executive office (I actually work out of a church youth center when I'm not at the gym), I don't drive a Ferrari, and I never pose with my arms crossed wearing sunglasses. When I'm not working, I am with my family. I am you, maybe just a few years ahead and a few more hard knock business lessons learned.

I welcome you to email me at any time.

There have been so many mentors that spent time with me that never asked for anything in return, people like Seth Godin, Mike Boyle, Ari Weinzweig, Tom Plummer, Tom Platz, Brent Gallagher, Vito La Fata, Pat Rigsby, Trina Gray and Todd Durkin.

I want to return that favor to you.

My personal email is vince@gabrielefitness.com.

My assistant won't get back to you, I will.

PART 1: THE BIG PICTURE STRATEGY

CHAPTER 1:
Your Member Avatar

For many years, we were the go-to facility in our area for training youth athletes.

Everything in our facility was geared toward that population. The look, the feel, the equipment, everything.

Getting new athletes in our doors was easy; it was crystal clear who we were and who we helped.

At the same time, I realized I was paying for a facility 24/7 so it's probably best I train adults too.

That's kind of how I treated them: a secondary market to our athlete program. The adult program started to grow by word of mouth and after a while, I started to realize we were in the middle. Our revenue was 50/50. I didn't really plan for this it just kind of happened but there was a problem.

We went through an identity crises and floundered trying to get the right message out to our community.

We had a website that, one day, had a 14-year-old kid deadlifting and, the next, a mom that lost 30 pounds.

It confused the community and it made the job of marketing our business very hard.

It was not until we made the decision as to who our primary market truly was that we got out of this conundrum. We chose moms and dads, ages 40-60, to be our bread and butter.

We were no longer a 50/50 split, we were an adult training facility and moved almost all of our resources to this primary market.

One of the deciding factors for this is we found it very hard and labor intensive to continue to reload all the athletes we
were losing each year, not to mention the small window of time these kids have in their day and the massive amount of activities they have as well.

Here's Some Upsetting News You May Not Realize:

Gyms lose close to 25% of their athletes each year. Even if you do a great job, at some point they will leave for college! The odds are stacked against the athlete-only training facility and that's why you see some pretty famous names that have closed their doors.

If you are going to create the freedom you want, you better pick the right market to focus on.

For me and for what I wanted for my business, I chose the adult market as it was the best chance to create a stable business model that would last for the long haul.

We still train youth athletes, but only in limited hours when we would not get many adults anyway.

It's now a secondary thought to our adult program and we never let it get in the way of our focus on growing the adults.

We had to make some big changes such as creating different websites and social media channels. We stopped training teams in our facility, which was a decent revenue bump but was inconsistent and required the entire gym. We took away sessions for athletes in the evening and opened them up to the adult members, even though we were making money in those times with athletes.

We put a much bigger emphasis on making our facility super clean. All the equipment we purchased was with the 40-60-year-old person in mind. Most of our events switched from things like youth speed clinics to adult nutrition hacks seminars.

You need to decide who your main target market is and set your business up for that market.

Once you decide who that is, you need to know everything about them.

You need to know where they live, what they do, how many kids they have, what their hobbies are, what's the one big thing that keeps them up at night, what are their biggest challenges and fears, etc . You need to become an expert in your main target market.

For the 10 best questions to ask yourself about your Member Avatar

Visit https://ultimategymguide.com/resources

Creating the profile

Once you answer these questions about your target market you need to create a profile client.

We call ours Frustrated Frank, or the female version Frustrated Francine, a completely different story than the one that follows.

As you can see, we even break down our primary markets into two separate profiles and we run our marketing separately to these two very different beings that happen to live in the same home.

Frank is a 50-year-old man that lives about 10 minutes from our facility. He is a lawyer that pulls in over 250K/year. His wife does not work and is also a member of ours in the morning sessions.

He has 3 kids in Middle School and one in High School, 2 out of the 4 of them train in our sports performance program. He loves golf, going on cool vacations with his family and plans trips to Canada to hunt and fish every year.

He is frustrated that his high stress job does not give him a lot of time to exercise and because he is so busy, he grabs food on the go. He wants to be a better role model for his son but just cannot find the right groove to get his health back on track.

His clothes are too tight and he's concerned about going up another pant size. He sets New Year's resolutions every year, but always fails by the end of January. He is confused by all the information out there and just wants someone to dumb it down and say "eat this, do this in the gym, show up at this time."

He values personal attention and relationships. He wakes up every morning with lower back pain and then sits in a chair all day. He feels like he is in a cycle he'll never get out of. Whenever he tries to start working out, he injures himself because he tries to train like he did when he was in high school, because that's all he knows.

He sees his ailing father and fears he is going down the same road. He is frustrated that his sex drive is also not where he wants it to be and it secretly lowers his confidence which impacts him in all areas of his life. He needs a solution, but just cannot find one.

After reading this, you probably feel like you know a lot about Frank. You can probably start to think about what would open Frank's eyes if he saw an ad for a gym.

It's definitely not a $10 per-month special membership.

It's probably not a picture of a guy with an 8 pack as that would just frustrate him more.

It's definitely not a picture of you!

So what will make Frank stop at you? What will make him say this is for me?

What will make him decide that this is exactly what he needs?

We're gonna answer this in the upcoming chapters; for

now, go ahead and create your perfect client, who is your Frustrated Frank?

CHAPTER 2:
Using the Right Bait

If you want to catch a striped bass, you better not use corn.

The entire goal of your marketing message is to get your target market to read an ad and say "this is for me."

The right bait is made up of 2 things:

1. What makes you different
2. Your offer

What makes you different?

When I first started, I was the only gym in town like mine.

I was the only one that had turf, prowlers, blast straps and a glute ham raise. None of the other gyms had this stuff. I thought it was what made me different and, for a while, I was sort of right.

Then, all of a sudden the crossfit boom hit. I was getting a call a day asking if I do crossfit. Their gyms looked just like mine. Then even the big box gyms like Lifetime Fitness, a five-minute drive from my facility, started to do the same type of training, using the same equipment I was using. The worst part: they were so much cheaper than me.

The things I thought made me different were very easy to copy and people were doing just that.

When I look back now, those things I mentioned earlier certainly made me different, but it was not the thing that brought us success.

What was bringing us success and what brings us success today is very hard to copy, in fact it's pretty much impossible. I welcome a gym to move next door to GFP and try, it will be a bad day for them.

When I ask this to fit pros in my mastermind, there is usually a dark eary silence. Many are just so deep in the day-to-day that they have not even considered the things that truly make them different from the guy down the street.

This is a key ingredient in your marketing and needs to be prominent on your website, promotional materials, content strategy and finally in the brain of you and your team when having conversations with potential members.

The easiest way I have found to discover what makes you different is an exercise called the Three Differentiators.

The exercise is to come up with the three things that truly separate you from everyone else.

It's possible for another gym to do one thing like you do, however, you need to find the three things you do that no one else does.

Take some time and brainstorm all the things that you do that would potentially separate you from other gyms.

It could be your customer service, the way you hire trainers, the proprietary system of training you created, the energy in the gym, etc.

Create a big list and then start to chip away. The goal is boil this down to three things
The key is to be able to say no one else does these three things like we do.

Our Three Key Differentiators at GFP are:

1. Positive Friendly Coaches and support team

2. Simple Training System

3. Family Like Atmosphere

Your Unfair Advantage

Whatever you decide your three key differentiators are, always remember people that can copy most things but they cannot copy the way you treat your customers. They cannot copy the feelings and emotions you bring into people's lives.

The best thing you can do to truly differentiate yourself is to have the goal of being the best gym in your area at customer experience.

Shoot, I would aim for being the best business in your area at customer service. It will not be that hard to do as the majority of businesses simply do not provide quality customer service.

If you try to compete with equipment or exercises its not

going to last very long. People long for connection and they long for their status to be improved.

The way you treat people may be all the differentiation you need.

My advice: Have everyone on your team read the book How to Win Friends and Influence People, it's the best place to start.

Your Offer

One of the massive mistakes gym owners make is their lack of an offer.

The least effective offer, in fact, is really not an offer at all. It's putting your name, logo, website and phone number out there and praying people do something with this.

Take a look at the ads other businesses in your community take out, they'll look exactly like this and I've been guilty of this myself.

You need to give your target market a reason to contact you, a reason that will move them down the buying line.

They need something very specific to take action on; they need to see it and say "this is for me."

The offer could also be a free info guide, report or workshop, but the real money is made when they schedule an appointment to come to your gym.

The focus of this chapter will be building out your trial

membership, the ultimate offer for a training gym.

We have had best success with a 30-day paid trial, but there are many options such as 15-day trials, free week, free sessions, either way you need to give people a reason to take action. A trial membership gives people that reason.

These could also come in the form of 6-8 week contests or challenges. We will be discussing these in detail in later chapters. These can be lucrative if done right. However, I do feel running challenge after challenge can get stale and start to disrupt your on-going memberships.

The key to successfully marketing these trial memberships is speaking exactly to your target market.

Beefing Up Your Trial

The trial price should be roughly 50% less than your lowest membership option, i.e., if your lowest option is $199, then your trial should be around $99. This is not an exact science and trial and error should be your best judge of your trial price.

Too many gym owners skimp on the trial. They feel that since they are charging less money, they should give less during the trial. Massive mistake.

The trial is a test drive. When you go to a dealer to test drive a car, they put you in the exact car you may buy. They don't say, "well this guy is only doing a test drive so bring around the jalopy." They want you to experience the actual car you may buy and, many times, they put you in the loaded model so you possibly fall in love with the heated seats, the sunroof and the v8 engine.

The same strategy should be used for your trial membership.

Here is an example for what we offer during our 30-day trial:

- Free Goal Setting and Nutrition Consultation
- A personalized 30-day nutrition and fitness roadmap
- 2 in-Body Scans
- A 1-1 personal training session
- Up to 12 small group personal training session
- Unlimited access to our Fat Blast class
- 4 small group Pilates classes
- Our hard copy recipe guide
- A fascial stretch therapy session

Our trial is loaded and it's why so many people take us up on the offer.

Advertising Your Trial

As mentioned earlier, if your target is men and women ages 40-60, it would make a lot of sense to separate the marketing message. This allows you to get much more specific with your copy, images, video, etc.

The mechanics of your trial will stay the same, only the marketing message changes.
Here is an example of one of our Facebook ads that

targets only men.

Notice the exclusivity of the ad. We say we are looking for 20 men.

It's very easy for them to take action by sending us a message with just their email. No question about what to do.

We don't direct people to our website for more info or put our phone number on the ad. We only want them to do one thing.

Take a look at the image. It's not a shredded dude from men's health. It's a normal guy that trains with us. People want to see themselves in the images of your marketing, at your facility (much more on this later).

We have a college kid come to the gym a few times a year and take pictures for us to use on our website, our content and our ads. It costs us next to nothing, but probably delivers a monster value as the image is one of the most important aspects of your ad.

Here are Kennedy's six principles from his course Magnetic Marketing, a highly recommended resource:

1. There will always be an offer
2. Give them a reason to take action now
3. Clear Instructions on what you want them to do
4. There will be tracking and measuring
5. There will be follow-up
6. Results rule

Guarantee

I never did this for many years because I lacked confidence and feared someone would take us up on this. What a baby I was.

A guarantee does not have to be to lose 20 pounds or your money back. The guarantee can simply be that they will get value from being at your gym or their money back.

Gabriele Fitness
Written by Mike Salvietti Fitness LLC [?] · February 13

Right now, We Are Looking for 20 Local #Men Who Want To Jump Start Their Health And Fitness.

If that's you, you'll get a completely customized program and 30-days of VIP Training Experience Here at Gabriele Fitness at a huge discount.

Spots are limited so apply below.

L.FACEBOOK.COM
Huge Opportunity For Berkeley Heights Area
We Are Looking for 20 Local Men Who Want To Jump Start Their Health And Fitness Before The New Year.

Apply Now

Chapter 2: Using the Right Bait

I have a guarantee for my mentorship program and it's if you don't walk away with a ton of value and several strategies to help your biz grow, I'll break out my checkbook and fully refund you in addition to your hotel.

I don't guarantee you will make a certain amount of money as that is truly dependent on you going back and doing the work. I can only control the information I give being simple and easy to implement, which gives you the best chance to succeed.

> Want to check out the exact Guarantee we use for the Gabriele Fitness Trial Membership
> Visit https://ultimategymguide.com/resources

CHAPTER 3:
The Execution Plan

The Execution Plan is how you take all the tactics you do for marketing and then organize them so they get implemented.

Planning is useless without execution and the Execution Plan is the map to the party.

A Execution Plan prevents you from what I call squirrel marketing, which I have been very guilty of in the past.

Squirrel marketing is you reading an article, getting an idea or hearing something someone else is doing and you doing it yourself. Sometimes this can effective, but it's not a predictable and reliable strategy.

The Execution Plan is best done in December to prepare for the upcoming year, but this is not a necessity.

The Execution Plan Jam Session

Block out about 2-3 hours a month with your team before the next quarter.

Talk about the things that worked well to bring in new leads last year/quarter and decide what you will be definitely doing again.

For example, every year we run a holiday card promotion in November and it has crushed every year. There is no way we won't do it again, but there is a time sensitivity to it. We want the cards to go out the Monday after thanksgiving as that's when people are hot to trot for buying gifts for Christmas.

We hand-address all the envelopes and that takes time, we write a new letter every year, we re-print the cards, etc.

Having this on the calendar signals us to starts getting this stuff ready a few weeks before.

After that, fill in the events/strategies you are going to use broken down into categories. Here is what we use but you may have different ones.

- Evergreen Strategy: Stuff you're going to do all the time
- Contests/Challenges: short term programs
- Core Events: Events that you host/run
- Joint Ventures: Partnering with other local businesses/programs
- Community Events: What you're going to do in the community
- Holiday Promotions: What holidays will you do something to bring in new members

Timing is very important in marketing and the calendar helps us do that.

HUGE Marketing Mistake

Putting all your eggs in one basket. Depending on one marketing media for all of your marketing is a mistake and will catch up to you eventually. We built a seven-figure business doing everything above EXCEPT Facebook ads. Everyone thinks Facebook ads are this magic bullet, but Facebook ads won't be here forever. Your ability to run an event at your gym and get belly-to-belly with your customers surely will.

Once all the categories are filled in you need to put this on some sort of calendar.

I really like a huge whiteboard calendar in the office where you run meetings. The whiteboard calendar gives you a full glance at your entire year and will be very effective at making sure you do what you said was important in December.

Having a backup on a hard drive in some online calendar program is probably smart too.

In our December mastermind, we all bring our whiteboard calendars in and go through this exercise as a group. Lots of great ideas are kicked around and everyone rolls up their calendar and leaves that meeting with a year of marketing planned out. It's a very liberating feeling.

> **Want more info on my Mastermind?**
> Shoot me an email at vince@gabrielefitness.com and put Mastermind in the subject.

Here's a sample of our Q1 marketing Plan

January

Evergreen Strategy: Facebook ads driving trial membership 3K, Facebook Content 1 post/day, Instagram content 2/day, Email 5 days a week

Contests/Challenges: NA

Core Events: Stroke Charity workout

Joint Ventures: Upper Deck and Pure Email promos

Community Events: Healy Silent Auction Basket donation

Holiday Promotions: NA

February

Evergreen Strategy: Facebook ads driving trial membership 3K, Instagram content 2 pics a day, Email 5 days a week

Contests/Challenges: Sweepstakes Launch Core Events: Speed Demo

Joint Ventures: Pure Email promo, Paddle tennis promo

Community Events:

Holiday Promotions: Valentines day trial 1 day sale

March

Evergreen Strategy: Facebook ads driving trial membership 3K, Instagram content 2 pics a day, Email 5 days a week

Contests/Challenges: Foolproof fat loss, Speed Week

Core Events: Sleep Seminar

Joint Ventures: Pure Email trial promo, RYS lead magnet

Community Events: NA

Holiday Promotions:

Please note: This is for my business and this specific plan should not be copied. Your marketing plan really depends on the size of your business, how much you want to grow, the available budget and the bandwidth available from you and your team.

The format, however, is a winning one and you can simply follow this well-rounded plan to generate consistent leads to your business.

CHAPTER 4:
Your Marketing Scoreboard

I had been an advertiser for a local online newspaper. I had a tough time seeing any real return on my investment. I terminated the relationship, but recently got a message that they left my ad running for 6 months after I terminated because they just forgot to take it down. The funny part was, now I know it was the right move to terminate it because I didn't even know the ad was running!

What gets measured gets done. Everything you do to bring in clients should generate a return. If it doesn't, you need to stop doing it. I have made this mistake and invested in things I would consider marketing that I had no idea whether they were a worthwhile investment. If you cannot see the results, you need to stop it.

Getting Your Lead Goal

Knowing how many leads you need to get in order to hit your membership goal might be the most important number in your business.

Let's say you want to go from 50 members to 100 members this year.

We're going to use a 2% attrition rate, meaning you will lose about 12 members over the course of the year.

Typical training gyms usually run around 2-3%.

If we start at 50 members and lose 12 then we're going to need 62 new members to hit 100 total.

This breaks down to about 5 new members a month.

I am going to use a conservative percentage and say that you convert 25% of all leads to full memberships. To clear this up further, think of you converting 50% of leads to trial memberships and then 50% of those trials to members.

This would mean you need 20 leads a month to get 5 new members a month.

Your focus is now on those 20 leads a month; the earth is off it's axis if you don't get 20 leads, go get it!

Tracking Your Leads

I'm a pretty even-keeled dude, but you want to know what would make me bite someone's head off?

Not tracking leads.

It's shocking to me how many gym owners do NOT do this.

This is the most basic yet overlooked principle in marketing: actually tracking where the heck people are coming from.

Having a very simple sheet at the front desk or on a spreadsheet is imperative to keep track of where new customers are coming from.

Failure to do this puts blinders on you. You won't know what is working and what isn't and that could mean lots of your valuable time and hard-earned money wasted.

Here's what you need to track:

- When they came in(date)
- How they came in (source)
- What they came in for (specific service or product)
- What the result was (what they did)
- Get their contact info (email/phone/address)

Create a spreadsheet with the following info on it, preferably in Excel so you can easily see the history.

Then, fill out this sheet 100% of the time you get a lead.

No excuses, no misses. Track. Every. Single. Lead.

> **Want to skip this exercise and just swipe one? Hit up https://ultimategymguide.com/resources for a sample lead tracking sheet.**

Cost Per Lead

Tracking your cost per lead is an essential number for each marketing channel you decide to use.

Let's say you spend $1,000 on Facebook ads and that generates 100 leads, your cost per lead would be $10. You can track your cost per lead (CPL) one of 2 ways:

1. Individual Marketing Channels

By tracking how much you are spending in each marketing channel (Facebook ads, print, etc.) and how many leads have come from each channel, you can get more accurate information on where the leads are costing you the least as well as which marketing channel is getting you the most leads.

The downside is of course that this can get complicated when you have multiple marketing channels going at once. Don't worry though, we will simplify this for you as much as possible in Chapter 7.

2. Global Marketing Budget

This is essentially taking your entire marketing budget across all platforms and dividing that by how many total leads you generated across the board.

This works well for some just because it's so simple and easy, but you get less accurate data than if you did the first method and might be spending money in places that aren't profitable or necessary.

Luckily we will be covering the only paid advertising you need to do in order to see massive success in Chapter 7.

PART 2: THE TACTICS

Back in the late 90's when I played football at Temple, we had a tradition called the O-line fishing trip. My best friend's dad was the captain of a fishing boat in Atlantic Highlands, NJ; it was one of the highlights of our summer. Picture this: fourteen 300+ pound men all piling onto this boat for a day of fishing. It was always funny to see the guys from the inner city that were ferocious human beings on the football field be so scared to bait a hook.

Here's the similarities between marketing and fishing. When we went on that trip, the only time we caught a fish was when one of us had our lines in the water. Never once did a fish just jump in our boat.

That's how you need to think about marketing. Your pole needs to be in the water… all the time.

There were many times I would cast my line and then nothing would bite. Then I would move 5 feet over and bingo, I'd catch a fish.

I will go over the most effective vehicles for generating leads and the one thing you need to know is most of them work if your clients are looking at that vehicle.

It may take a little more time or a little more tweaking, but all the vehicles have the ability to flood leads to your gym. You just need to keep your line in the water, pull it in quick and then cast it right back out either in a different spot, with a new pole or different bait.

Fitness professionals are notorious for trying Facebook ad for two weeks, getting nothing and then saying that Facebook ads do not work. Like fishing, marketing is a process of trial and error. Here are the tactics you can deploy.

CHAPTER 5:
The Referral Engine

Hands down the best way to get highly qualified new members to your gym is through referrals. Referrals are so much easier to sell into a membership because part of the job is already done by the member that told them about you.

Here is the number one thing you need to do to generate referrals:

Create an environment that creates ultra-inspired and enthusiastic members.

Walt Disney said, "Do what you do so well that people can't resist telling others about you."

We call this passing the coffee test.

Many times, a mom will come train with us in the morning and then meet a friend for a cup of coffee afterwards.

The key to success in your business is dependent on what happens in that conversation.

The conversation goes like this: Friend: How was your morning?

Your Member: OK or fine or good with a sort of high pitch voice.

This will NOT get your gym any referrals
Let's try again:

Friend: How was your morning?

Your member:
Awesome! I worked out at Gabriele Fitness in Berkeley Heights. I've been going there for a few months and you know me, I have tried everything, but these guys are on another level.

Everyone remembered my name the first week I was there, their trainers are super friendly and really know their stuff, in fact you know that shoulder problem I always had, they make sure I don't do anything that injures it and all of the trainers know I can't press weights over my head.

When I started they gave me a really easy nutrition plan I have been following and I've lost 20 pounds of fat since I started. I even know the weight I lost is fat and not muscle because they have this special scale they use. Walking into the place is like drinking two energy drinks.

It's always clean, the music is awesome and their trainers really get you excited about being there. I have to be honest I don't always want to go because I'm just not crazy about exercise, but I have not missed one workout because every time I walk in the door the energy just gets me going and I feel awesome for the rest of the day.

They also gave me this super cool metal card that's good for a 30-day trial membership, you want to check it out?

Chapter 5: The Referral Engine

This is the goal, this answer passes the coffee test and the chance of that person coming to the gym is very high.

The Point of Sale Referral

Once a member commits to a contract, they are the most excited and in the best frame of mind to refer you a friend or family member.

Not doing this is leaving money on the table.

We give them a black metal card that's good for a 30 day trial membership and ask the following question.

Who would you like to give this to?

They normally will give you a specific name when you frame the question like this.

The mistake is asking "Do you know anyone?"

The answer is usually I'm not sure or I will get back to you. The question above frames it so they think of a very specific person and the key is getting that name in the meeting.

Once you get the name, the follow-up is crucial.

Send them an email that night thanking them again and cuing up the introduction by doing something like this:

Hey Danny,

First off congrats on becoming the newest GFP member. We are more than grateful for you and cannot wait to see your success over the next year.

The best compliment we could ever get is someone telling their friends and family about us.

We are truly grateful to you for introducing us to the people you think would benefit from our program.

Below is a sample email to send to your friend Mike you told me would want to use the card we gave you.

If you have any questions please do not hesitate to call me.

Karen

P.S For introducing us to your friend, we'd like to give you a gift, stop by the front desk and pick up any supplement you want.

Hey Mike,

I just became the newest member at Gabriele Fitness in Berkeley Heights.

They specialize in helping people like us get more energy, lose weight, sleep better, eat better and live longer!

When I signed up they gave me a free 30 Day Free trial to give to a friend.

I want to give this to you so you can give them a shot. I cc'd Karen from Gabriele Fitness on this email, she will reach out and get you started

Hope to see you in the gym!

P.S. They have a ton of success stories on their website www.gabrielefitness.com

If they do not give us a name, email this the next day:

Hey Danny,

Just checking back to see which one of your friends or family you'd like to give the free trial membership.

Let me know!

Karen

The Holiday Referral Card System

This is one of the most successful things we do every year the week after Thanksgiving.

We give all of our members a card that entitles the bearer to a free 30-day trial membership. It is designed for them to give as a gift to a friend or family member.

We get large 8x11 envelopes and hand write the address. We put in a letter from me thanking them for being such valued members and tell them about the card they can use as gift for a friend. We also tell them that they get 25% off anything in our store. Here is a copy of the letter we send.

Dear GFP Family Member,

We hope you had an outstanding Thanksgiving with your family and friends. We could not be more grateful to you for your dedication to the GFP family.

We are so proud of all the hard work you put in each time you come to GFP. I know you are setting a great example in your home by your dedication to your health and fitness.

Thank you so much for trusting us, it is an honor to be chosen by you to keep your health strong.

In order to help you get a head start on your holiday shopping, we have enclosed a Trial Membership card for you to give to a friend or family member valued at $499. This card is meant for new members. Each card is good for 30 days of our adult fitness trial membership.

Please give the gift of fitness to anyone that you chose.

As our gift to YOU.... bring this letter in with you and receive 25% off any supplements, equipment or GFP gear.

Great members equate to a great year! Your support allowed us to make a living with what we love doing.

We appreciate the time you spend with us every year, and look forward to serving you, your friends, and family for years to come.

Thank you for being a member here at GFP!! Please feel free to call me anytime.

Vince

Follow-up is key here too. We send an email a few weeks later that looks like this:

Subject: The Card We Gave You

Dear John,

A few weeks ago you received a package from us in the mail that contained a card for a 30 Day trial membership for you to give as a gift this holidays season.

Just curious, who are you going to give the card to?

Please let us know by December 15th first as the offer will end soon.

Thanks! The GFP Team

CHAPTER 6:
Grassroots Marketing: A Forgotten Art That's Timeless

I built a million-dollar gym without running any online marketing.

We were kings of grassroots marketing.

I had a marketing guru, that never owned a successful business, tell me he could get me all the leads I wanted from Facebook ads.

What this marketer does not understand is the power of the handshake. The power of communicating belly-to-belly with the people in your community.

I love Facebook ads, they have made life much easier and more predictable, but I'm not sure it will have the impact it has today in a few years. It will be something else.

The absolute biggest mistake you can make is putting all of your marketing eggs in one basket.

Grassroots marketing in your community is cheap and can bring very big returns, most people just don't do it right.

The power of word of mouth, the referral and most

importantly a system to drive these things.

There is a ton of results waiting if you do this stuff right.

If you're reading this book you most likely own a gym in a local suburban community.

There are hokey local town fairs, 5K races, high school football games on Friday nights, chili cookoffs, beefsteak dinners, tons of fundraisers for schools, churches and local charities.

There is a ton of power in being present in your community and the ones that overlook these opportunities will be at a disadvantage.

The issue here is that all small local gyms have tried this stuff.

They put an ad in the church bulletin, they got a table at the 5K race, they set up a talk with a local moms group and most of time....crickets.

So, they move on and say that kind of marketing doesn't work.

These opportunities work, but they just need to be approached in a different way, a way that follows the principles mentioned earlier from Dan Kennedy in Magnetic Marketing.

Here is a list of potential things you could participate and how you can maximize it:

Sponsorships

Most of the time these are an absolute waste of money. They promise signage, your logo on a t-shirt with 50 other businesses and your name mentioned once over the loudspeaker. It's perfectly designed for large business to park their extra advertising dollars that they don't care if it goes into a black hole or gets lit on fire.

But for us, these dollars matter. These wasted dollars could be going to our kids' college fund. Instead, they evaporate and there's nothing to show for it.

Unless…

You do things a little different. Everything, especially on the very very local level, is up for negotiation. The key to successful sponsorships is creating your own rules.

We never pick the gold option or the silver one. We tell them we would like to make a donation to their program of a specified amount. We tell them we don't need our logo on the shirt, we don't need signage and we certainly don't need our name mentioned.

What we ask for is direct email access to their list. This is valuable because local sponsorships such as a PAL or High School Booster clubs are the exact type of clients in our target market. It's the perfect place for us to be, but only if we can get direct access and ask for direct responses.

It's important to be clear that you are NOT asking them to give you the emails of their list. This makes them very uncomfortable and pretty much makes you a spammer. You want them to send the email. The email is from

them, on your behalf.
We will create a very specific exclusive offer to their list. This could be a live event at our facility, a special offer for them to try out our gym or some type of content based article that leads them to opt in for a free resource that's of value to them.

Check out a textbook version of this.

Their initial email to me (names and locations have been removed to protect privacy):

Hey Vince,

I wanted to reach out to you regarding an opportunity to Sponsor a Platform Tennis Tournament. My Club hosts a tournament every February bringing in the top players in the game.

I figured it would be a good opportunity for you to Market your business to people who might not know about it.

Basically, what we're looking for in a sponsorship is $500-$1000 and that will get you marketing through brochures, signs, and even a table of your own if you'd like.

It also gives you Air Time on a live stream which typically get around 10k-20k views on the weekend. If this is something that interests you, feel free to give me a call or text.

I would be more than happy to chat. If this isn't something up your alley, no problem at all. I am trying to gather local businesses and see if anyone is interested. Hope all is well with you. Talk soon!

John

My response:

Hey John!

Thanks for your email.

Unfortunately, we no longer do sponsorships in exchange for branding type promotions.

We would however participate in a joint venture where we'd contribute $500 in exchange for 3 emails sent to your list about a special discounted program we would create for your members.

Let me know if you would to explore this options.

His response:

That would be awesome!! Here's what I can do. I can send something out to our members of the club as well as to the whole list of players in the tournament. And I'll even go a step further to send it to the Platform Tennis Association. That way I can cover as many people as possible. Let me know what you think!

Perfect. A win for both of us. They get their money and I got direct response style marketing.

So you may be thinking $500 is a lot of money for 2 emails.

Chapter 6: Grassroots Marketing: A Forgotten Art That's Timeless

There were a few factors here.

The people in this club were in my exact target market in terms of demographics, geographic and psychographics. This makes this opportunity a hotbed for my gym.

For $500, if we get only one member it was well worth it as the lifetime value of a member for us is $4,320.

Knowing the lifetime value of one of your members is critical information you need to justify spending money on marketing.

My friend and marketing guru Paul Reddick always asks:

How many times would you spend to $500 to make $1,000? The answer is as many times as possible.

Without this mindset, someone that invests $500 and only gets one clients considers that a failure when in reality it's a massive victory, pending the lifetime value exceeds the marketing spend.

In addition, when we have them send the email we include a landing page. When someone visits the landing page, we now have the ability to re-market to them.

Nothing much happens from an ad on a poster with a picture of your business card.
If you like setting money on fire, then do the same marketing as big businesses do.

The reality is this, most people say these things don'twork but they do…if you do it right.

Getting a Table at a Fair or a 5K

I shoot to do as many of these as possible. When I first started, I did them all...myself. I spent many fairs sitting there with my wife staring at each other. It wasn't until we changed our strategy that these things started being very valuable ventures for us.

When you set up your booth you need a few things:

1. Something really cool to raffle off that has value

If you raffle off a hoodie with your logo or a tub of protein powder, the line is going to be small. No one cares about this stuff because they probably don't even know your business yet, so why would they care about a hoodie with your logo on it?

They most likely don't even use protein powder. These things also have a low perceived value so it won't entice them to give you their email just to enter the raffle (the key ingredient to a successful booth).

We have had great success with giving away a 30-day trial membership at our gym. At a $500 value, it's big enough that people won't think twice about entering for a chance to win it.

2. Create something fun to attract people to your booth

We have done vertical jump testing, stretching on a massage table, mini lectures, football tosses and, most recently and very successfully, our fake weight picture venture (shown next page).

I've done many booths where I just slapped some flyers on the table and hoped people showed up. If you're going to invest the time, do it right. Make it an experience.

NOTE: I personally do not go to these things, I am an introvert at heart and opt to send my most outgoing people to run these events. That being said, I was at every booth with my wife Vanessa for the first seven years of our business. You need to earn the right not to go.

3. Have a direct response handout

Create a flyer that simply has 2 things:

a) Customer Showcases. This should be a picture of the market you're trying to attract and the story of their success at your gym. You will see that ours has two separate customer showcases, a man in his 50's and a woman in her 50's. These are the exact type of members we're looking to attract.

b) An offer for a trial membership at your facility. Clearly outline what they get in the offer and be crystal clear on what they should do to take action.

> **Want to check out an actual email we would send to their list in a situation like this?**
> **Visit https://ultimategymguide.com/resources**

When you get it, note that it's not pretty. This flyer took us about 10 minutes to create. It's focused on what you want them to do; make it clear. This is what direct response marketing is all about.

Follow-up after the event.

This is where most completely drop the ball.

1. Select the winner and email them to come in to redeem their free-trial membership.

2. Load all the new email addresses into your database and send them a "thank you" email telling them they unfortunately did not win the trial membership. In that same email, offer to have them come in for a discounted trial membership instead. Be sure to put some urgency on the offer.

3. Add the new email contacts to your follow-up campaign to continue marketing your trial membership to them.

4. Add the unconverted email to your newsletter email list.

Joint Ventures

I want to tell you about the time I sold my wife…

We had just moved into our new location and I got a call from a girl that's owns a local dance school.

They were looking for someone with a fitness background to train their dancers. The school was a very well run business and had hundreds of kids training with them.

Hundreds of kids meant a ton of parents all within our target market.

I had heard some of the other businesses had tried to do a joint venture with them with little luck.

When they asked me if I knew anybody only ONE person came to my mind.

My wife.

My wife Vanessa, despite being a pilates instructor and stretch therapist, was a lifelong dancer.

She was the perfect person.

She started training their dancers a week later and it has opened up an incredible joint venture.

Since so many of the dance moms and dads now know her from all the buzz of this new relationship we have seen a very strong uptick in our adult fitness program from the people that drop their kids off at this school.

They have also been super kind and sent several emails (something I negotiated in the sale of my wife) to their list about our trial membership program because we put together a special package for them.

This is one example of several of these types of relationships we have leveraged to help build are business.

The key is to look for other local business that compliment what you do and have your target market at their fingertips.

It's very important that these relationships are not and do not get one-sided.

Before I asked for anything from the dance school in terms of email promo, we solved a very big problem for them.

Finding ways where you can provide value is crucial to success.

Here are some ways to win with joint ventures:

Make a list of all potential local businesses or organizations in your area that would create a mutually beneficial relationship.

Here are some ideas: dance schools, batting cages, sports club teams, chiropractors, physical therapists, massage places, restaurants, sneaker stores, running clubs, equipment stores, acupuncture, nutrition coaches, orthopedic surgeons, coaches, youth league commissioners, etc.

The biggest question I get is how I have gotten so connected with so many of these people.

Use these 3 strategies to meet the people you need in your corner:

1. Cold call and ask their advice
2. Pay them
3. Get introduced to them

The Cold Call

Here's the famous story of how I got a pipeline of referrals from a knee surgeon that wouldn't stop and how I created a relationship with one the best physical therapist in the world, Charlie Weingroff, who eventually was the reason I got selected to speak on the Perform Better tour.

I wanted to learn more about ACL reconstruction because we had a few random clients come that were recovering from ACL surgery.

I knew from word of mouth that this doctor was the goto surgeon in our area.

I cold called his office and told him I had just opened up a new gym and had gotten a few clients that were recovering from ACL surgery.

I told him I was looking to learn as much as possible and asked him if I could watch one his surgeries and afterwards ask him a few questions.

Impressed with my willingness to learn and grow, he said yes.

They dressed me in scrubs and I watched a 45 minute ACL and about a 2-hour shoulder surgery as a bonus. These surgeries are more like construction sites, the hammering and sawing that went on blew my mind.

At one point, the doc called me over right by the person's knee being operated on. He was like "check this out Vince, this is the torn ACL." It looked like crab meat.

All of the sudden, I looked down and my feet were in a puddle of blood. It was an experience I will never forget. It was awesome.

After that point, he knew if this personal trainer was willing to take a day to watch surgeries, they must know what they're doing.

Then it happened: a flurry of ACL Post op clients, all happily paying close to $1500 a month for the specialized service I was offering, post-rehab ACL training.

When the Doc recommended them to come to us, they came.

We went on to run seminars together for close to 8 years after that.

Sometimes you just need to pick up the phone and call.

The key to starting this relationship was me asking for his help so I could help others.

People respect that. I was not there for my own personal gain, I was there to better serve my clients.

When you ask for help in an instance like this, you are positioning them as the expert.

You are basically conveying how smart they are, your respect for their knowledge and experience and how much you want to learn from them.

This makes people feel great about themselves and, in turn, they think of you in a very favorable way.

Pay The Man

A second way to get in the door is to pay. I started to educate myself on training ACL athletes and sought out Charlie Weingroff, one of the world's best physical therapists. I hired him for the day to teach me everything he knew on ACL post rehab training.

This was before he was pretty famous so the rate was affordable. I then hired him again to come back to run an in-service for our team. Then I started sending patients his way.

We developed a pretty good friendship and still are regularly in touch today. None of this happens if I didn't pay. You want to get in the door, show them the money.

The final way to start these relationships is with a strategy that's just about as proven as gravity to get a response…

The Email Introduction

When you find a business on your list that would be a great joint venture, think about someone you know that could intro you to the person in charge.

There was a massive lacrosse club that was the top dog in the area, they had hundreds of kids.

I had wanted to work with these guys for years and even had a meeting with them once that went nowhere.

Enough time had gone by and I wanted to take another

stab at it, though I honestly didn't know if they even remembered me.

I saw on social media the owner of the club (I'll call him Seth) was doing a project with one of my best friends from high school (I'll call him Mike).

I called my buddy Mike and asked him if he could give me an introduction to Seth, he happily agreed.

He sent an email to Seth that went something like this:

Hey Seth,

Great seeing you out in China last month. I want to introduce you to my great friend Vince Gabriele(CCD). He owns a gym in Berkeley Heights and is honestly one of the best trainers I have ever seen. I think it would be a great partnership for both of you.

You guys take it from here,

Mike

Since Seth knows I am cc'd, he would be totally disrespecting Mike if he did not respond to me.

Getting someone to send something on your behalf is a surefire way to at least start the conversation. Cold calling can work, but this is so much more effective.

The key is finding the connecter that knows them well enough and then asking for the introduction.

It's important to note that you may need to tee this up

by telling your friend exactly what you want them to do.

That script would go like this:

Hey Mike,

Can you introduce me to your buddy Seth that owns XXX lacrosse club? Just send him an email introducing me and CC me on the email, I will take it from there. Cool?

As you can see, I was close enough to Mike to get right to the point. In a more formal situation it could look like this:

Hey Mike,

Hope all is well. I was wondering if I could ask for your help.

I know you are friends with Seth, the owner the XXX Lacrosee Club. I think we can really add value to the performance side of their business and help them become an even more competitive club.

Would you be willing to introduce me to him via email?

Just send him an email and CC me, I will take it from there.

Sound good?

1. Build your Angel List

When I first started training kids out of the back of my pick-up truck, I came across an angel. I had just moved back from California and a guy that went to my high school had just taken over the high school football program of one of the surrounding towns.

He was older than me, but we stayed in touch periodically. Once he got the job, he was my first visit. I told him I was looking to open an athlete training business and wanted to help his team out.

I went to weight room and trained his team for free almost everyday after school.

He had been around strength and conditioning for a long time but the way I coached the kids and different stuff we were doing really caught his eye.

I earned his trust as a strength coach very quickly and he started talking about me.

Word spread and things started to happen.

This resulted in my first group of paid athletes. He let me use his field for the training so I had no overhead. It was about nine kids, one of them was his son who of course came for free.

It was interesting how much pull this guy had for being a new coach. I think it was because the program was so bad they looked at him as the savior even before they had a great season.

With luck on my side and this football program continuing to win, the community started really getting behind this movement.

They started to win more. Then they won a state championship, then another and then another.

I was his guy. I was the guy responsible for getting his player in incredible shape. He told everyone, everyone.

Field hockey followed, then lacrosse, then basketball, then the youth athletes came, then parents of the athletes for fitness training. It was like a series of dominoes falling from all the people that came to me all through one man.

My business exploded quickly and he was a huge reason why, hence my nickname for him, my angel.

I thought about the business I could have if I created more relationships like that, that is exactly what I did.

This is your Angel List.

It's a list of people in your community that you have created a very trust-based relationship with and now have direct access to their community of people who are all in your target market.

We created close to a ½ million dollar business in my first year from these strategies.

$0 spent on paid marketing. Just hitting the pavement creating these rock solid relationships.

There are a few keys to creating Angels:

1. You need to stand out

You must be really good at what you do, get results and demonstrate a fire and passion for helping the people involved. In this case, I spent every waking moment learning about making high school football players stronger and faster.

He saw I was on another level and this created instant trust. Don't expect to get any of these types of relationships without a burning fire and some really solid measurable results. Sometimes you get lucky and results come in the form of state championships. I got way more credit than I deserved, but I took it, I had a business to get off the ground.

2. You must give before you get

What value can you bring. For me it was offering my expertise for free. I honestly feel this is the best way in the door. You don't have to do what I did and go crazy training an entire team for free.

You can offer a free seminar, workshop or demo that benefits their audience, offer a special exclusive discount on your services or just to sit with them and brainstorm ideas that could help their network. Always go into these relationships thinking how can I had value to the people this person helps.

When I started, the majority of my angel list was coaches, athletic directors and youth program coordinators but they can can even be clients, local business owners, teachers, doctors etc.

3. You must ask for their help

This is where so many people fail. They earn their trust but then never take advantage of something that has massive potential.

They can survive without you offering free services and value added things discussed above, but you cannot without members.

Once you build the trust, the next question is asking for their help.

Here is an example:

Dear coach,

It's been great working with your team, you have a great group of kids in your program and I am loving the opportunity to work with them.

I was wondering if I could ask for your help.

I am starting an adult fitness program and think it would really be helpful to the parents of your athletes.

I have put together a special package for them and was wondering if you are willing to send a series of three emails to them to let them know about it.

Would truly appreciate your help on this. If you are able to help me with this just reply and I will get everything set for you.

I want this to be as little work for you as possible so I

have already drafted the emails for you to send to them. To make it easy for your parents. I created a special page where they can register for the program as well.

Just reply back and let me know.

Thanks!

Maintaining Angel Relationship

When I was communicating with the knee surgeon mentioned earlier he asked me if I ever trained adults. I said, of course we do. He asked me to start working with him 1-1. This was huge and I was nervous. Here was one of the best surgeons in the state and a former NFL head orthopedic doctor and he was trusting ME to train him!

The first night I trained him, he went through the workout and everything went great. Then I almost blew it. I was stretching him on the massage table and all of sudden I heard and felt this thundering rip coming from his hamstring. My jaw dropped. I thought I tore it off the bone.

He too was a little confused.

I asked if he was ok and he said yes. I then asked what the hell was that! He looked back, still confused but kind of smiling, I don't know. It was a comical exchange and we both kind of laughed about but my heart was in my throat

Despite almost ripping his hamstring off the bone, he continued to train with me.

Then something weird happened. We started getting a daily referral from him, they just kept coming in, one by one. It was crazy!

It was because we were on his top of mind all the time because he was coming to our gym, talking to our other coaches and meeting our members.

My gym was just in his head and he trusted us so he told everyone about it. Everyone.

The best way to solidify these relationship is to get your angels training in your facility. The majority of angels will live local so it makes sense for them to train at the place they are telling people about.

I do NOT recommend giving them free training BEFORE you have a relationship.

I have given them free training or have comped their children to keep the relationship going but only after a solid relationship is built. If you offer to do this too early it's viewed more so as bribery.

Staying in consistent contact with your angels is key. Don't let four months go by and then ask them for something. Keep in touch by asking about them, their health, their kids, their teams, etc.

I shoot for one contact a month with my best angels if they are not training with us.

Sending them gifts is a great idea too. I always hook them up with the latest GFP gear and even send them things at birthdays and holidays.

One of our extreme angels was the director of a VERY large youth program and was responsible for countless amounts of new members. He was always helping us out by sending emails on our behalf.

He also happened to be a sales expert that spent the day with us working on our sales system. I called him our sales yoda and brought him a large yoda statue that still sits in his office today. Now every time he sees the yoda, he thinks of Gabriele Fitness.

A great book to read on giving cool gifts is giftology by John Russin.

Once you develop a sound relationship and build large amounts of trust there really isn't much they won't do for you.

CHAPTER 7:
Core Events

A local business that does not run events at their facility is leaving money on the table. Yes you can make it but this book is not about making it, its about thriving and creating the life you want to live.

Events take some work but the key is getting it down to a system so its less and less work while the rewards become greater and greater.

We have had tons of experience in our 10 years and have helped dozens of other fit pros put on awesome events that have made a massive impact.

Contests, challenges and holidays

When we had our first fat loss challenge many years ago, If you don't know, a beefsteak dinner is where they bring out endless supplies of filet mignon on a piece of bread. Since everyone was in the fat loss challenge, no one was eating the bread.

As the night went on, the tables were accumulating largepiles of bread and people started playing this game of who had the bigger bread pile. Its was the talk of the night. We were the focus of pretty much every conversation at that dinner, you can't buy that kind of advertising.

Chapter 7: Core Events

These events can be total game changers when used appropriately. They can be destructive to your membership if abused.

Running a constant challenge always looks like your sole focus is bringing new members in and it leaves your current members saying Remember me? I'm the one that's been paying you $300 a month for the last 3 years!!!

That being said, running fat loss type challenges that include both inside AND outside members at some strategic times of year can be lucrative.

The purpose of these events are to stimulate sound referrals, give your members a kick in the pants and build up your back end sales, i.e. supplements, gear, etc. People are looking for opportunities to get in shape and short term programs like these are proven to be great lead generators. People are simply looking for the next thing that's going to get them what they want, these challenges are smart ways to get them in your door. After they are in, get some success and you earn their trust, they are prime for becoming full time members to your facility.

These also serve as great motivators to your current members. Them being involved in the challenge brings a much greater chance of them bringing in a friend to do it with.

These things also get your business talked about among the community.

Here are some examples of events like this that have been successful:

21 Day Reset: This is designed to be a value add for our current members and build up back end sales.

6 Week Foolproof Fat Loss: This is a referral generating program where we put out a cash prize for the team of two that loses the most body fat. We have created a very specific nutrition system for them to follow during this program.

Biggest Fat Loser: Another cash prize program where people get together in teams of five people in order to gather the most points in a system we created where workouts, healthy meals, massages etc gave them points. The teams of five needed to have a least two non-members.

Sweepstakes: A free giveaway designed to give people a chance to win a high value program. This is highlighted in detail in an upcoming chapter.

Here are the times where these types of programs are very effective:

Mid-January: For obvious reasons, everyone wants a fresh start, ignoring this is foolish. If you are not going to run a challenge than up your ad budget in this month to capitalize on the people that are looking to make this their year to get back in shape.

Late September: I believe this is one of the best times but unfortunate is ignored by most gyms. The holidays (Thanksgiving-New Years) are only about 6 weeks long. From Memorial Day to labor day is close to 12 weeks, double the amount of time to get out of shape. There are graduations, bbqs, summer vacations, travel, 4th of July is in there too. There is so much time and so many things to potentially get off track with your health and fitness. People are dying for a jumpstart once the kids get back to school. You need to be there with an opportunity.

Mid to late April: This is pre-memorial day. The trigger that they will need to be on a beach in a few weeks! This is a great time for a shorter term challenge (14-21 days).

February: This is a hidden gem and if you run a challenge in February, I'd hold off on one in January. This is the strategy we use at GFP because we simply know we are going to be busy in January, we don't need to use a challenge to get a bunch of leads. We just up our budget and run our evergreen ads and we historically have done very well in January.

Most people start the year with these resolutions that this year they are going to get in shape. But the stats are not on their side. 90% of new years resolutions fail by mid-January.

A February challenge is their second chance, a lifeline. Hence why we always have performed very well with February challenges.

The Sweepstakes

We had a really tough year a while back.

One of our key trainers left the industry, we had to let someone go that was pretty much running the show and it was the only year on our history that we did not grow.

But I really think we just got complacent. We had a great run of growth and thought it would just keep churning. It didn't.

We needed something to set us back on fire.

Since we were getting our ass kicked we met as a team and said we need to do something different, something that's going to put a burst of life into our business.

When you have an off year, everyone feels it. The team feels it, the clients feel it and you become obsolete in the community.

With the help of a former client of mine, Neil Horowitz, who ran social media for several NHL teams, we came up with a solution. Many times, going outside of your direct network is what you need to do.

This solution put a spike in our revenue column we had never seen before.

It put a surge of energy through our team. It flooded our gym with new members. It reinvigorated current members and got many of them back on track.

It made us the most talked about business in our entire community.

This is one of the most important concepts in this book, call it whatever you want, buzz, interest, going viral, publicity, doesn't matter.

If you want to take your business to the next level, you need to get people saying "what the heck is going on down there at....?

There needs to be interest in what you're doing, something so great it's going to set your gym on fire.

At the time of writing this book we are in launch mode of our 5 th time running our sweepstakes transformation challenge.

It has been the most successful marketing event in the history of our company, by a landslide.

Here's what we did:

We put out an email and ran Facebook ads that said we were giving away four spots in a six-week transformation challenge. We promoted it for about two weeks.

Hundreds of people filled out a very detailed application, we interviewed eight of them and selected four.

We followed the four people in a documentary type fashion and showed the community everything they were doing at our gym.

The people that went through the six weeks crushed it! The entire community was tuned in to following these people, it was amazing.

The amount of people that started to train with us after these six weeks was staggering.

This program will help you:

1. Create massive success stories you can use for years on end
2. Build your email list because giving something away of this magnitude really gets attention
3. Generate a surge of energy into your gym
4. Get the entire community talking about your gym
5. Get several long term new members

Here is a look at the exact email we sent to launch this program.

Subject: [Six-Week Free Giveaway] Doors open! It's go time!

http://gabrielefitness.com/sweepstakes-2018

<u>Our annual Six-Week Giveaway is now live and accepting applications.</u>

Once the application window is closed, we will select four lucky participants.

Each winner will be getting six weeks of custom, hands-on training and nutrition coaching, with a real-world value of $1499.

So don't miss out, fill out your application now, here:

— The GFP Team

P.S. If you are already a member of GFP this is a great way to get your friends, family or loved ones on the same page as you, so share this link out as best as you can (we recommend Facebook).

> **Need help implementing this into your business? Shoot me an email at vince@gabrielefitness.com and I will get on the phone with you and talk you through it . . . Free."**

Holidays

One of the other things I learned from Neil Horowitz was to take advantage of holidays like Black Friday and Valentines Day. I always thought that stuff was cheesy and for businesses that competed on price. Boy was I wrong. Something like a Black Friday sale is just an opportunity for your target market to take action. Remember back to one of Dan Kennedys Magnetic Marketing Principles: there will always be an offer. Holidays give you that opportunity to theme that offer when people are already pre-programmed to buy.

Here is a list of potential holidays to take advantage of:

- Mothers Day
- Father Day
- Valentines Day
- Thanksgiving
- Christmas
- Memorial Day
- Labor Day
- Easter
- Veterans Day

- Jewish Holidays
- St. Patrick's Day
- Presidents Day
- Cinco De Mayo
- MLK Day
- Daylight savings time
- Spring Break
- Christmas Break

You do not have to have a sale on your trial membership for all of these, but rather theme something to sell or some kind of offer around some of these dates. For the record, we do not do something on all of these holidays, but we decided what we were going to do at the start of the year.

One great example I heard from one of my mastermind members was taking advantage of when kids had off school. Parents are always looking for stuff to put their kids in when they have a day off because kids these days just don't go outside and play for the day. They need something structured. It's a shame, but it works for our businesses.

They promoted some free workouts for kids in the community to train in the middle of the day. They now have new people in door they never had before and could sell them into their youth program and also sell their parents in their adult program. Its was brilliant!

Seminars

Running seminars at your gym may be one of the best decisions you can make for your business.

It will position you as the expert in your community.

Simply being on stage and hosting an event puts you in a small category of people willing to do this.

Public speaking is one of the biggest fears among people and the ones that get good will have tremendous success.

Being an expert in your community is more valuable to your business than being famous on a national level. No local potential members will read or care about your article on T-nation about deadlifting. They only care about themselves and the value in it for them.

Some topics have included: nutrition, stress, ACL injury prevention, concussions, hormones, sleep, goal setting, recipe sharing, golf performance, meditation, low back pain relief, detoxification, mindset, etc.

Another awesome idea is partnering with other local professionals such as doctors, chiropractors, acupuncturists, physical therapists, massage therapists, chefs, sleep experts, etc.

This allows for double promotion and gets people to your location that you would not have gotten without them.

A final idea is bringing in a paid speaker that is a celebrity.

Here is a checklist when thinking about promoting your seminar:

Decide how many weeks you will promote the event (3-6 weeks does the trick).

Decide who will promote the event for you.

Write the emails for them to send(usually a three-email series).

Create the landing page.

Decide on date and times(be sure to check the local event calendar in your community to make sure it does not conflict with other events that could impact your attendance.

FREE is great

We never charge to host seminars and we instruct our mastermind members to do the same.

To get more people in the door for these seminars, you need third-party endorsements in addition to your own list and social media promo.

Here's a short list of Local organizations that may help promote your seminar:

- PAL
- PTA
- School Districts
- Rec Departments

- Education Foundations
- Booster Clubs
- Club Teams
- HS/MS Teams
- Chiropractors
- Nutritionists Physical Therapists
- Moms Groups
- Boy/Girl Scouts
- Pools
- Restaurants
- Churches

All these organizations may willingly promote a free seminar that adds value to the people on their list. As mentioned earlier, an angel could be very helpful here.

They view a free seminar you as giving back to the community and helping people, when you charge money, they view you as a business looking to make a profit.

> **"Want to check out our seminar landing pages? Visit https://ultimategymguide.com/resources"**

1. Capture Emails via Landing pages

Landing pages are great for collecting emails, one of the biggest reasons why you should do seminars, they build your email list.

Not all people that register will show up, that is pretty standard.

The key is keeping in contact with them as they have

already shown interest and make take action on another opportunity.

2. Get them excited about the event to improve show rate

When we started sending content-based emails to the people that registered, our percentage of people that registered versus showed up skyrocketed, no joke.

Think about a very short article, video and a gentle reminder that they have reserved a seat at your seminar.

Build the excitement and make it a big deal.

Some people don't even remember they signed up for these things, they need to be reminded.

Make an Offer

We always provide an offer at the event that ties back into.

They get a one sheet with letter from me with an offer.

Discounted Jumpstart for adults, free assessment for athletes.

We try to schedule assessment's at the event, this is when they are the most hot.

But…

We also email them the offer that has an explanation.

We follow this structure.

One, three, seven days after the event, we email.

> **Want to take a look at the exact Power Point we use to sell our trial membership from the stage? Visit https://ultimategymguide.com/resources**

Charity Events

I stood in front of a crowd of close to 80 people not knowing if I was going to be able to hold it together.

I was recounting the story of when I told my dad, 17 years ago, I wanted to be a personal trainer. I thought he was going to beat me. I thought he would say I was crazy and that I needed to get a real job.

I went on to tell them that he did the opposite. He embraced it and later even loaned me the money to buy the equipment for my first facility. He was proud of me, but prouder of the amount of lives that had been changed from 10 years of business at Gabriele Fitness.

I held it together, but many in the audience did not.

As they wheeled my dad in during my talk, I saw him smile. He did not know what I was saying as he cannot speak or understand language, but I could tell he was proud.

It was the first time my dad had been anywhere since his stroke. He was either in our house or at the rehab center.

This was our first event of the year to raise money for stroke.org. It was a large group training session where people gave a minimum donation of $25 to attend.

We promoted it hard through email, Facebook, Instagram, joint venture blasts, targeted shares and word of mouth.

I choose stroke.org because of my dad, my high school football coach who passed earlier in the year and for the many tough conversations I've had with our members when they were going through the awful challenge of taking care of a family member that had had a stroke.

It was close to me, close to our members and close to our team (we also have had several team members affected by strokes).

It was something I know the community could get behind.

The first event we raised over $10,000, not bad for one workout in a local gym.

We set a goal of raising 25K for the year specifically for stroke.org.

Charity events run by you and your team are win-win situations.

You help people in need and your business gets attention from people that normally may not of ever come to your gym.

Here are a few options for how to structure these events.

We typically run 2-4 per year usually in the form of a large group workout but there are several other ways you can get creative for these events.

1. You can pick one charity and do everything for that charity for the rest of the existence of your business.

2. Select one charity of the year where you chose one organization and run events towards a financial goal for that charity (my preferred method).

3. Run Various events choosing a different charity each time.

Chose a charity that will bring the community together.

Before we chose stroke.org we did a few events for a local teacher that had cancer, the community was really pumped up to help her and it put us in a great position to help and get new members to our gym.

Running events for charity are easier to market as more and more people are willing to help you get the word out, either with email blasts, shares on Facebook or even physical signage in their stores.

At the end of the charity events, we sweeten the pot for the attendees and create an opportunity to make more money for the charity.

Normally there will be a combo of members and non-members at your event. It's important to urge your members to bring their friends to the event, explaining the more the merrier. A great question to ask your members is "who are you bringing with you to the charity workout on Saturday?"

Offer a discounted trial members to the non-members. Tell them you are going to donate the entire amount of what they pay for the trial back to the charity.

For your members, offer them to purchase the same discounted trial they can give to a friend as a gift. Again, donate 100% of the money back to the charity.

The Speed Demo

I know many guys that follow my stuff training athletes so this is for you.

I'm going to break down an incredible strategy for getting more youth athletes into your gym. Many gyms struggle with marketing for this population and having a tool like this gives you the power to get new, highly qualified athletes in your gym.

We have used this method several times with great success and actually can clearly track back close to $20,000 in business from one member alone. The total revenue from all the demos we've run is well over $100,000.

Bottom line: THIS WORKS.

Here's what you need:

1. A relationship with a local influencer

If you are active in the community one of the big things you should be doing is building relationships with influential people. When I first opened GFP, I pushed hard to get to know coaches, youth directors, athletic directors and athletic trainers in my community.

These people hold a very important key to bring athletes to your door: an email list. Step 1 in having a successful speed demo is having a minimum of one of these relationships that is strong enough that they will send an email for you to their list. I have found these speed demos work best with the younger populations (3-8th grade).

Although a phone call is best and my preferred method when asking the coach to promote one of these events, you can also use an email.

Hey John,

Hope all is well with you and your family. I wanted to touch base and see if you would like to offer a free speed training demo to your athletes.

Let me know,
Vince

Notice the email is very short and to the point. The goal is to just get a YES.

This only works if you have a current relationship and have regular contact. Sending an email like this to someone you have not spoken to in three years or someone you don't know will probably not work.

Again, a phone call is your best bet to ask for something like this.

2. Planning the event

Once you get a commitment from your local contact to promote the event, you now need to plan it. Here is what you need to decide. It may help to ask the coach what he thinks would be best for his audience.

Where: The absolute best place to have this in in your facility. If your facility is not equipped or you do not have a physical location then ask permission to use their local field to host the event.

When: We have had the best success having these events on Saturday or Sunday mornings. You want to avoid weekdays as parents are busy and may not be able to attend.

3. Create A Landing Page

These are super simple to create, but after you decide on the best day and time with your contact, create a cool visually appealing landing page. There should be only one thing for them to do on this page: enter their name and email to register for the demo. That's it! Just know that not all of the people that register will actually show up.

This is normal with free stuff but totally ok. You now have the contact info of an interested local parent. They may not come in this time, but now they are on your list and you can market to them on a regular basis. This is one of the great benefits of this program because it acts as a local list builder as well.

This should be set up so when they register they are put on an email list for this specific event.

4. Write the emails for the coach to send

One of the keys here is making this as little work for the coach as possible. Do not leave it up to them to pick the dates to send, create the email subject line and write the actual email. Most coaches have very little marketing experience.

You do everything. Send them exactly what you want in the email, but write it from the coach that is sending it, NOT YOU. The subject line FREE SPEED DEMO has worked very well for us.

Include the basic info of the event in the email and put the link to the landing page. Give them the exact date you want it sent. I like them to send three emails a week apart leading up to the event.

5. Set up reminder emails

Since lots of people register for free stuff but many time do not show, we need to get out in front of this. We will send several email reminders to the people that register building excitement for the event.

We'll ask them to arrive 10 minutes early to give them a little urgency. Make it very clear that this is NOT a drop off session and parents are strongly urged to watch the event.

The key to making sales in these events is impressing the parents, which hard to do if they are not there. In these emails also tell them there is limited space in these events and if they have to cancel to please call you.

What this does is create another opportunity to make a connection. If this pushes them to call you to tell you they cannot make it, it gives you an opportunity to offer them a free consultation at another date.

6. Run the event

9:50-10 AM

Greet parents and kids as they enter, try to avoid any awkward silence. The parents and kids will be somewhat nervous, introduce yourself to each kid and parent.

Be sure they fill out all necessary legal and contact info (Email, phone and address).

Send kids back to Interns to start warm-up.

10 AM- 10:05 AM

Initial Parent talk (5 mins)

Tell them everything that's gonna happen, make them feel comfortable.

Introduce yourself; tell your story and what their kid will take away from the event. Talk about your philosophy and how it's different.

Tell them about the opportunity to sign up for a free assessment after, hand them assessment coupon and flyer for program.

Ground Rules for parents (nicely and funny): No coaching your kids, no using the equipment, stay off the turf and in the weight room.

10:10-10:30 AM

Take over session from Intern and do the drill that most demonstrates how kids can improve speed and/or agility. This is the most important time as the parents will be seeing the head coach instruct the skills.

10:30-10:45

Talk to parents (Ask them questions about their kid, as them to point them out to you, tell them a positive thing and one thing they need to work on).

This is a time where easy drill should be used that are productive and fun, but and intern can run on their own i.e. tennis ball sprints, cone cut drills.

10:45-10:55

Nutrition Lesson (ask parents to come close and listen, be sure to send them home with some type of physical handout from this lesson).

10:55 to close

Address parents, ask about any final questions. This is where you recap the structure i.e. times, days and answer any questions they have specifically about the program.

If they would like to sign up for an assessment have them see Ellen/Karen, they should be standing by you with the clipboard.

7. Follow up emails

The best case is that they take you up on your offer at the event. If they don't, we still have a great chance with an email follow-up. We send an email that night, three days and sevens days later to push the offer we proposed at the event. If they do not take advantage add them to your regular list to stay in contact with them.

If you train youth athletes, just know a very disturbing stat:

You will lose a least 25% of them each year. Even if you're the best coach in the world, they go off to college. They stop playing sports, they get too busy with all the other stuff in their lives. Its very hard to have a stable base of athletes year round.

Having tools like the free speed demo does not solve this problem but gives you a tool to get new athletes to your door to fill the bucket that is unfortunately leaking!

CHAPTER 8:
Email Marketing Machine

It shocks me how many fitness professionals do not use email.

Email is cheap, instant, allows a great platform for engagement and you can reach a ton of people with one click.

Here is why email is so important and it may be more important than social media.

You do not own Facebook or your Facebook account.

I see posts all the time from fit pros saying Facebook shut down my account or would not approve their ad.

You're always at the mercy of the bots or a nerd behind a computer screen that doesn't like your wording on an ad.

The rules are always changing with social media making it tough to keep up.

People that put all their eggs in the Social Media ads basket may run into some serious challenges.

The key to email is consistency and sending content that adds value.

When I tell rookie business owners that we send five emails a week they usually cringe and respond with something like "aren't you just bothering people?

Wont they just unsubscribe?" I respond by saying that people who weren't going to buy anyway are the ones that unsubscribe.

You need to send emails that add value to people's lives. In the fitness facility world, it's things like success stories, recipes, motivational emails, funny videos, nutrition tips, etc.

All these things add value to people that are interested in living healthier lives. Therefore, we send and will continue to send for the foreseeable future.

Here's what you need to do:

Have an email list that has all of your members, past members, prospects and anyone else in your universe that could either refer you a member or become a member themselves.

Find a service like mailchimp or constant contact to start. We currently use active campaign and love it, but it it's a bigger investment. If you just want email to start than the programs above are fine.

Email the list regularly. Start with a minimum of once per week and increase as you have the bandwidth. Send it on the same day and at the same time.

Provide value.

Don't send endless emails about things like cancelling due to snow or trying to hammer them with a 15% discount before you've provided any value. Your emails should do 4 things: Educate, entertain, inspire and make money.

The majority of our emails are valuable content based emails but always have a call to action. The CTA is usually to our trial membership, an event we are having or even just a response t to engage a conversation. When we periodically blatantly sell something, it usually works. On Black Friday, we sold 25 Trial memberships at $99 each from four emails. If we never provided value, the results would not be as promising.

Not too Long.

Fit pros have a tendency to be very long winded. Keeping them short is probably your best bet. This does not mean that a long one will not work it's just that people are busy and if you can deliver value in a short amount of time they will probably come back more often.

Legendary copywriter Ben Settle described it like this. Treat the length of your email like a women's skirt, you want it long enough to cover the deals but short enough to get your attention. He recommends 300-500 words.

Don't send one really long email newsletter

When we first started, we sent one email a week that was chock full of the exercise of the week, member of the week, an article, and some other stuff I cannot even remember. It was too overwhelming and gave too many different things to read.

When I get a long email like this I usually do not read it. You want to provide people short valuable content that is easily digestible.

A giant email newsletter also lowers the frequency of emails you will send.

Meaning, you will only be on the minds of your potential customers once a week. If you took all this stuff and made each section a separate email you now creative more opportunities for you to be on their mind and more potential engagement opportunities.

> **Want to check out the exact emails we use to promote our Black Friday Deal?**
> **Visit https://ultimategymguide.com/resources**

Growing your local email list

There are several ways to grow your local email list and many of the strategies in the core events and grassroots sections will help you do that. For instance, running a seminar or getting a table at a local 5K are all opportunities to get new people on your email list.

You can also create longer articles, reports, infographics, short books, manuals or checklists and use them as lead magnets.

It's pretty simple

1. Create the information product you think your target market would be excited about enough to give you

their email for it. We had great success with a recipe book we created. Your gonna want to find a graphic designer to create a cool looking cover to attract more eyeballs .

2. Decide how you want to deploy these, you can run an ad on Facebook or get a joint venture to email their list about the gift.

3. Create some type of landing page where it describes how it will benefit them and have a place to collect their name and email.

4. Send them the gift, it's usually a digital product but can be physical.

5. Create a series of follow up emails after they opt in the the gift and ultimately try to get them to come in to your gym, these should be automated emails that are set up in a program like, click funnels, active campaign or infusionsoft. If they don't take you up on the offer now, they may later when they are ready. Keep them on your list and deliver value as stated above.

CHAPTER 9:
Social Media Content

The final evergreen strategy is your content on social media. We use Facebook and Instagram but others can work well too.

There is an entire world of people that are simply not ready to start training with you.

They need to be educated. They need to be reminded. You need to be there when the problem you solve moves to the top of their to-do list.

As mentioned above here are the three things your content should do:

1. **Educate:** This is where you do a video on a beneficial stretch to help a tight back, give them a recipe, talk about what they should be eating after a workout, before, etc. You are making them smarter.

2. **Entertain:** Making people laugh is a sure-fire way to get attention. Using humor in your posts will drive engagement and overall just make people feel good about your brand. We filmed a mini movie call Breakfast Cops that pretty much went viral in our community. It shows our trainers dressing up as cops looking for members that eating like garbage.

> **Want your ribs to hurt?**
>
> **Check out Breakfast Cops Episode 2 Visit https://ultimategymguide.com/resources**

3. **Inspire:** Write something from the heart that will get your people shaking their heads. My high school football coach recently passed away. He had a huge impact on my life and was an icon in the community. He transformed hundreds of young boys into men. I wrote a tribute to him and packed in a bunch of lessons along the way.

When you write something that parents sit down and read with their kids you know you hit it right.

The sum of these three things need to answer the question, does your content make people feel like a better person? If you can answer yes, then you are on a great path.

Make them smarter, make them smile, make them cry and you'll win.

Many struggling gym owners I speak with on the phone tell me that they don't have time to post on social media(Then I see them posting crap on their personal Instagram account of them squatting and it makes me boil. If you have the time to film selfie videos of your 225 squat you can post once a day to add value to your members.

Content in the categories above (Educate, Entertain and Inspire) are very easy to find if you have a gym that is currently training clients.

The content is right in front of you.

Walk around your gym and just look around.

People are exercising, sweating, smiling, laughing, motivating each other.

You'll see people that have lost weight, that's a story.

You'll see someone that touched their toes for the first time.

You'll maybe see someone that beat cancer.

You'll see someone that did their first chin-up or push-up.

You'll see someone deadlifting 135 for the first time (which to a 40-year-old mom is a huge).

It's all happening right in front of you. The best part: These are the people you need to be showcasing in your content.

The reason being is that **the people you are trying to attract are the same people in your gym right now.**

If your market is women in their 40's, you don't want to show a high school football player deadlifting 315 on the trap bar. Those women do not care.

But, if those women see someone just like them in your post or, better yet, see a friend or colleague, now we're talking.

We have had many members that have come in for a

consultation and the way they heard about us was by seeing one of their friends like their post.

They contacted us through the paid ad, but the reason they gave was their friend liking the post.

This is why you need both paid ads and social media content.

Some action steps:

1. Have a camera on the floor with you and take pictures or short videos of all the things going on during your sessions, instruct your coaches to do the same.

2. Commit to making at least one short post per day of something happening at your gym that fulfills the 3 criteria. It could be something as simple as a woman in your gym doing a pull-up and tagging her in the post, telling her "great job!" and that you're proud of her. I am sure her friends will chime in.

3. Commit to one longer Customer Showcase post that tells the story of someone that had success. This should also be distributed by email.

Websites

One of my good friends and marketing Ninjas Colin McCarty calls this the grunt test.

Go to your website and see if it passes.

When you log in, does it immediately tell people the following in about 5 seconds:

- What do you do?
- How will it help me?
- How do I sign up?

Your website should be designed for one thing: to get people to reach out to you for a trial membership.

Local gyms make their big money on their main product, selling personal training, don't distract them with anything else.

Here are a few guidelines:

Be sure you have two opt in buttons for a trial membership above the fold, one in the center and the other in the top right.

Have an image or video of your target market.

Have a strong headline that tells people what you do. Create a 3 steps process for how it works at your facility.

Here is how we outline ours on our site:

Step 1: Come in for a free consultation
Step 2: Try a risk-free trial membership
Step 3: Join the GFP Family Include your 3 Differentiators too.

DO NOT

- Take up half of the website with your logo.
- Put a picture of you with your shirt off or in a bikini, no one cares about you, they care about their results, this crap scares people away.

CHAPTER 10:
Paid Advertising

When I first opened in 2008, I took a small block on the very top of the front page of the local newspaper. It was for a free trial workout to our Fat Blast Class; it crushed.

If I tried to take that ad out again, no one would answer my call because they are out of business.

Local newspaper have suffered greatly and have been replaced with online publications, which can be another marketing black hole, a topic for another day.

The reality here is paid ads work and they can be very easily tracked which is very good for tracking your marketing effort.

These days when referring to paid ads, I'm talking about ads on Facebook, instagram, google, youtube etc. If you have the option to do direct mail or take out an ad in the newspaper I would only do this after you have given these platforms an honest try. After all, these platforms are where your customers live everyday.

Who is in your ads?

There was a guy on a forum I am a part of ranting about how his Facebook ad wasn't working. He posted the ad and it was a ripped woman in her 20's.

The ad copy was toward moms and dads looking to get in shape, massive disconnect. The image was driving his target market far away from his gym.

If you are in your 20's or early 30's and there's a picture of you posing on your website or Facebook page with your arms crossed, take it down, immediately, you're scaring people away.

People don't care about you. They about themselves. The thing that's going to get them motivated to show up to your gym is seeing people just like them in your marketing.

You want them to say, if she can do it, I can do it too. They look at you and think you were born that way and eat boiled chicken and broccoli every meal.

If your target market is moms in their 40's, use a current member that had success with your gym that fits that demographic.

Don't show them struggling through the workout in pain either, get them happy and smiling, preferably with a group of their friends to show there is community in your gym. You don't want people to think you're running a torture chamber.

Finally, if you are one of those trainers that only wants to work with in-shape and motivated people, I have bad news for you. You're going to be poor. I'm sorry, but it's probably true.

For every in shape and motivated mom in your community, there are a 1,000 others waiting to be helped. By choosing such a small piece of the pie, you're putting yourself at a major disadvantage.

Customer Showcases and Testimonials

One of the challenges in running paid ads is that you are marketing to a group of people that do not know, therefore you have not established trust yet.

Most gym owners are not good enough marketers to build trust from an ad that talks about the key differentiators of their business and I'd argue that this is hard for most great marketers too.

That's why so many great marketers use testimonials. What your members say about your gym is simply just much more credible than anything you can say.

The Ultimate Testimonial

Let me tell you about the Ultimate example of social proof that flooded my gym with new members.

We had a woman named Cathy that participated in our six-week sweepstakes challenge (described in detail later in the this book).

Cathy did awesome during the six weeks as she lost 25 pounds and completely changed her life from a very unhealthy one to one that was motivating an entire community to get healthy.

Cathy was the typical mom that put other's well-being before herself and it showed in her lack of focus on her own personal health.

This is story of so many moms that have and are raising children.

She talked about in her videos and social media posts how she hated exercise more than anyone and ate Twinkies all day and never touched a vegetable.

She would always say:

"If I can do it, anyone can."

The story took over the community and the engagement on social media and in-person was something we have never ever seen. We called her our Jared, as in the Subway commercial.

She inspired so many people to come and train with us because she was the voice of hope and possibility. We could ever say anything to make this kind of an impact.

Now there was something a little special and different about Cathy.

First she had an amazing outgoing, honest, brash, loud and extreme personality.

Second, she was a true local. Born and raised in the same town as my gym, everyone knew who she was… everyone. Cathy was 10 times more effective than any national celebrity I would have had to pay.

She was the perfect person to sell our gym because she not only was smack in the middle of our target market, but she has an incredible story to go with it. The results prove this.

Paid ads are great places to use customer showcases. Whether they are written with a good image or a short video (1-2 minutes) they both have a strong impact pending the target market is right.

These are designed to tell the story of the success that person had at your gym. People are drawn to stories and when your ad is simply a story about someone just like them they will take notice.

How to Get Testimonials

One of the best ways to gather these stories is set a goal to get one per week.

We put a customer showcase out every Wednesday via email and social media, then reuse the good ones in our paid ads.

At our team meeting, we spend a portion of the meeting talking about the possible people we could use for our Wednesday showcase.

We reach out to them and ask if they would be willing to be part of our Wednesday showcase posts, almost all agree.

A huge mistake is not asking for fear of people saying no. Not everyone will say yes and I have had a few people ask me to take it down after they agreed to put it up. Nothing should deter you from moving forward towards gathering as many stories possible of the success of your members as it could be the most important aspect of a sound marketing plan.

Do this exercise for a year and you have 52 stories of happy, satisfied members you can use in your marketing.

Here are the questions we ask them when interviewing them for a customer showcase.

X = your gym name.

Where were you at (physically/mentally/etc.) before X?

Where are you at now?

What challenges have you overcome as a part of our family?

What accomplishments are you most proud of as a result of training with us?

> **Want to check out testimonial videos we use in our ads?**
> Visit https://ultimategymguide.com/resources

What are the biggest benefits you've seen as a result of training here?

What do you love most about X?

How does walking the doors of X make you feel?

What three words best describe X?

What would you say to someone who is considering joining our family, but is on the fence?

Who is running these ads

I do not recommend outsourcing all of your marketing to an agency, especially ones that focus on your logo, website and brochures.

Remember, one of Dan Kennedys rules: results rule. Many of these agencies focus on everything else except consistently bringing you highly qualified leads, the only metric that truly matters in your marketing.

I have worked with many of them and most do not understand direct response marketing.

You will see in the upcoming chapters that many of the strategies that work and will never stop working need to be done in house and take little marketing expertise so hiring an agency to do that stuff for you is a waste on money.

As the owner of your business, you need to control and completely understand the marketing, it's the most important job as the business owner.

That being said, you don't have to carry out every task yourself. Spending time learning how to run ads in programs like Facebook, Google or YouTube may not be the best use of your time.

Finding people that do this for a living is easy and its normally worth the money invested based on the return.

You can do it yourself, but I think as long as you have good communication with your ad manager and you have complete control over the copy the images, headlines, etc., you will be alright.

If you have the money to hire an ad manager that is also a sound direct response marketer, thenn go for it. This is the route I have taken because it gives me the time to do things, like write this book. They are not easy to find, but asking them who their marketing mentors are is a start. If they have never heard of Seth Godin or Dan Kennedy it might be smart to run other way.

There are 2 places that have proven effective for my facility and for my mastermind members.

I'm going to let our Director of Marketing at GFP drop some bombs about how to succeed with Facebook advertising. Like I have said many times, this is not the end all be all, but if you ignore the power of Facebook ads, you're missing a big piece. Hold tight, he's been referred to as a wizard with this stuff, take it away Mike.

Facebook Advertising: Your tool to compete with the big boys and beat them at their own game.

Hey… Mike here. I'm a former gym owner myself and current Director of Marketing at Vince's gym, Gabriele Fitness.

Undoubtedly, if you've made it this far in the book, you've likely had several "ah-hah" moments, coupled with moments of doubt and skepticism, and that's completely reasonable. That's because the stuff you are being taught in this book is, not only "uncommon knowledge" but likely goes against a lot of what you thought you knew.

This section is no different. By the end of this section I'm tasked with convincing you that you can not only compete with the big bad marketing budgets of the "globo-gym" down the street, but even beat them at their own advertising game, using less money, using the power of Facebook.

> **Disclaimer:**
> You will not be able to sit at the computer with this book next to uou and step by step, set up a Facebook ad. The platform is constantly changing so anything written here can change the very next day. That's why we keep an up to date video tutorial for you at https://ultimategymguide.com/resources

So why Facebook?

I'm glad I made you ask! Here are the top reasons why I know for a fact, Facebook ads are the best advertising for you to start with, no matter what your budget.

Facebook ads are Cheap!

There are 2 simple ways to gauge how expensive your online advertising is, how much it's costing perclick (meaning how much it cost you to get someone to click your ad) and how much it costs per 1,000 impressions (meaning how much it costs you to have your ad seen by 1,000 people).

According to very recent stats at the writing of this book, the average cost per click on Facebook ads in the US has been about $0.28.

Compare that to an ad on google, the average cost per click was closer to $2.32, a whopping 88% difference!

So what about the cost for 1,000 to see your ad? On Facebook it's about $0.80 – $1.00 on average, compared to googles average of $2.75.

But what's also really great on Facebook is that you can start for as low as $3/day. So no need to have a big budget to get going.

Facebook is Highly Targeted

With google ads, it's all about keywords. You basically show an ad to people based on what keywords they type into Google's search engine.

From there, you can narrow down a little bit further to age, gender and location, but not much beyond that.

Facebook on the other hand has thousands of variables you can target. Not only can you target people based on their locations, age, gender, parental status, sexual preference, relationship status and job title, but you can actually target people based on their interests and behaviors as well.

That's because Facebook tracks all of their users activity across likes, link clicks, comments, etc. So you can get super precise.

One fitness company named Orangetheory Fitness, at the time of this publication have grown to nearly a billion-dollar company thanks to hyper targeted ad campaigns towards affluent moms in a 5 mile radius of their gyms. That's quite impressive when you stop and really think about it.

Facebook has all the eyeballs

Right now, Facebook has over 2 Billion active users and 79% of all Americans use Facebook.

The second highest used social platform is Instagram, which is actually owned by Facebook and in fact, all Instagram ads are ran through Facebook.

Not only does it have the highest monthly active users, the average user logs on to Facebook 8x's per day and spends an average of 35 min per day on the social networking site.

Facebook ads are easy

Setting them up is a breeze and can literally take minutes to get up and running. As I mentioned before in this chapter, we even have a detailed video tutorial on how to set them up at www.vincegabriele.com/resources

The 4 Parts of a Successful Facebook Ad Campaign

In order to be successful with Facebook ads, you need to have a solid marketing plan of action that converts Facebook users into leads for your business.

Here are the 4 critical components you need in place to make this work.

1. Your Offer

You can't just throw up a Facebook ad telling people that you are an awesome personal trainer and that they should contact you to get in shape. Just like you covered in Chapter 2, you need a low barrier offer that has a high perceived value to entice people to give you their information.

2. Your Audience

Your audience is everything about your ideal client avatar as discussed in Chapter 1. You need to be clear about where they live, how old they are, do they have kids, how much money they make, etc. That way you can target only those people on Facebook with your offer, ensuring no random people see it that aren't a good fit demographically or financially.

3. Your Ad

Yes, the ad itself is just part of the puzzle. You need to have your ad structured properly to grab the attention of your audience, convey the offer properly and call them out to take action and give you their information.

4. Your Funnel

This is basically the series of actions that your prospect goes through to give you their information and come in to your gym to train with you. It's how you capture their information to follow up with them in a timely manner while giving them a clear expectation of what is going to happen and what they get.

The Anatomy of a Great Facebook Ad

Every Facebook ad has 5 critical components

1. The Ad Image/video

The ad image accounts for roughly 75%-90% of an ads effectiveness. That's A lot of pressure to rest on the image you choose!

When choosing an image you need to make sure of a few things. You want an image that portrays your ideal client in their ideal scenario of working out in your gym. The best way to do that is choosing an image of a client that is successful, that fits your ideal client avatar, training in your gym.

Next you want the image to stand out, by being very high quality (no crappy, bad lit smartphone pictures) and including colors that contrast with Facebook's newsfeed.

Lastly, you want the image to include someone or multiple people looking and smiling directly at the camera. That helps grab the attention of your prospect when they are scrolling Facebook and see eyes staring back at them in a photo.

2. The main headline

This is the big bold text that is located directly under your photo or video. Here is where you likely put your offer that you want them to click on.

3. Facebook ad description

This, in my opinion is the second most important part of an ad. This is the text that is located above the image/video. Here is where you get to call out your ideal client, describe in detail what you are offering and basically tell them what to do next.

4. Headline description

This is a small box of text located under the headline that reinforces what they get and what to do next.

> Want done-for-you Facebook as templates to copy and model so you can cut out any guess workand start profiting immediately?
>
> Get 6 proven ad copy templates at https://ultimategymguide.com/resources

Tracking The Success of Your Facebook Ads

In Chapter 4, we discussed the importance of tracking your Cost Per Lead from your marketing budget. To do this specifically with Facebook, you simply take the total amount of money you spent, divided by the total number of leads you got from Facebook. So if you spent $1,000 and got 100 leads, your cost per lead is $10.

But what's a good cost per lead? How do you know if you are spending too much per lead? How do you know if an ad is profitable?

To get these answers, you simply need to be able to understand how valuable a lead is for your business. This is not a theoretical number, but actually based on your sales and conversion skills, followed by your price point.

So let's say you only get 1 out of every 10 leads to come in and buy your offer and your offer costs $100. That means your value per lead is $10. So assuming you spend $1,000 to get 100 leads, but only sell 10 of them a $100 offer, that means you broke even, because each lead cost you $10 and every lead only made you $10.

Keep in mind though this is just a front end number, every one of those leads is a possible client paying monthly and also a referral source. So you don't always have to break even or even make money on the front end of your Facebook ads if you can afford to spend more to get the right people in the door.

CONCLUSION

After many years as a gym owner, I did not always appreciate marketing. I looked at it as a chore more than the most important aspect of my business.

I now spend the majority of my education on becoming a better marketer because I know that will be the one skill that will help any business grow continuously.

In my conversations with fitness professionals that own brick and mortar facilities, the most common frustrations are:

1. They struggle with generating consistent leads

2. They have to be glued to their business for it to be successful

3. They are not making enough money

4. They don't have enough free time to be with their family

5. They are always tired

I've been on the phone with gym owners that told me they desperately wanted to do things like have children, purchase a home or get married but didn't take action because of the unstable environment they were in with their gym.

This left them stressed, overwhelmed and many times looking for a way out of the fitness industry, an industry they once deeply loved.

I have seen a ton of great trainers get catapulted out of the fitness industry because they lacked the ability to stimulate sales for their business.

This book has the power to help you develop that skill but know that it will come over time, just like any other skill.

When you commit to becoming a great marketer, things will start to click, business will get a little easier and so will your life.

It's been an honor to go on this marketing journey with you.

As mentioned earlier, feel free to email me anytime with any questions at: vince@gabrielefitness.com

THANK YOU!

– NOTES –

– NOTES –

Made in the USA
Monee, IL
12 May 2022